CENTERFIELD COMMAND

Owning the Outfield

Skills, Drills, and Thrills

SKY BENSON

Copyright © Sky Benson, 2024

Except for reviewers who may use brief sections in reviews, no part of this book may be duplicated in any way without the publisher's prior written consent by any mechanical or electronic means, including information storage and retrieval systems.

View other books by this Author at: Vipublishing.com

TABLE OF CONTENTS

CHAPTER 1

THE HEART OF THE OUTFIELD

Critical role of a centerfielder.

On the softball pitch, a vast area of green seems to go on forever. The Centre field is in the middle of this green sea. This area is often mistaken for a lonely post. But don't let the quiet fool you. A type of player rules the centerfield: the centerfielder. They are the leader of the off-base runners. Their job is critical and requires a unique mix of physical and mental strength. Imagine a chess expert who can move very quickly. Now you know what a centerfielder is all about. Their speed must be the fastest on the team, and they must have arm strength like a gun. But speed and power aren't the only things that matter. The defense anchor is the centerfielder, who looks over the whole field. They're like the quarterback of the outfield—they call the plays, lead the other outfielders, and make sure everyone can talk to each other easily. When the batter hits a line drive into the gap, the centerfielder has to move quickly, reading the ball's path and choosing the best way to make the catch. It's always a game of waiting, a dance with the unknown. The duty goes beyond just catching fly balls. A natural centerfielder knows how the game works. Based on the count, the number of outs, and the men on base, they guess what the batter will do. They can set themselves up in a way that lets them cover more ground and keep the area as complete as possible. Every move in this game is like a strategy game of chess, where anything can happen. There is a lot of pressure. One mistake, like missing a catch, can cost the team a lot of money. Still, the best centerfielders do great when they're under a lot of stress. They consistently concentrate, like a laser, which lets them block out noise and move without thinking. They are mentally tough enough to get back on track after dropping a catch. Their confidence is unwavering, burning with the drive to do well. But playing centerfield isn't just about defense. They also add something insulting. They could be the player who set the tone with their speed and ability to hit the ball hard at the top of the hitting order. They can bunt to move runners along, steal bases to pressure the defense, and surprise everyone with a big hit when the team needs it most.

Think about how great the centerfielder is the next time you watch baseball. Do not be fooled by the area of the field that looks quiet. A player in the middle of that green area is a respected leader, a master of the game, and the real general of the outfield.

Perfecting your fielding mechanics

"And footwork."

You hit a line drive that sounds like a laser beam cutting through the air. As the centerfielder, you are the only thing to stop it. People in the room gasp, and the tension rises. You are relaxed and collected, though. There's nothing wrong with your body. You jump into action, making a blur of smooth moves, and catch the ball with a rewarding snap in your glove. Fielding with perfect form and movement makes all the difference between a heart-stopping moment and a routine out. Good movements are the basis of any great centerfielder. Your body's invisible language to the ball turns rough situations into smooth plays. The basic stance is where you should start. This is a balanced position with your knees slightly bent, your weight spread evenly, and your hand held high and ready. It is a platform that lets you act quickly in any way. From this position, footwork is the music that plays out. It's the moving lyrics that lead you to the ball. It's not about using physical force to get good at footwork; it's about being quick and accurate. Small, quick steps are the key. Think of a cat sneaking up on its food while being quiet and fast. Each step should get you closer to the ball while keeping your balance and control. There is a sure way to catch ground balls. As the ball speeds towards you, shuffle step toward the ball with your lead foot (suitable for right-handed people, left for left-handed people). Then, hit the ball with your glove down low and your legs slightly bent to soften the blow. Don't forget that a smooth glove change from your throwing hand to your catching hand is significant for a clean play. You need to take a different method with line drives, those screaming missiles. It would help if you had quick reactions and a strong core. Stay low in your stance and take a small step with your back foot toward the line drive as the ball comes off the bat. Your hand should be spread out, palm facing the ground, and you should be ready to catch the fast-moving object. Fly balls, which look like beautiful curves in the sky, might look like the most accessible balls to see, but you must pay attention and be in the right place. Here's where being excited comes in. To guess where the ball will land, look at the batter's swing and the direction of the bat. After that, move your feet to get under the ball. Keep your eye on the ball and adjust your position as needed as you backpedal easily with small, controlled steps. It takes practice to improve, and lessons are the best way to improve your mechanics and footwork. Here are some must-haves:

Cone drills: Line up cones in a square shape and practice moving your feet back and forth and side to side, just like you would for ground balls and line drives.

Tennis ball drills: Have a partner throw tennis balls at you from different directions to force you to react quickly and work on your glove transfer with a lighter object.

Fly ball drills: Hit fly balls at different heights and distances with a fungo bat to improve your tracking and backpedalling skills.

Being consistent is very important. Set aside time every day for drills, even if it's only for a short time. When you practice a lot, the proper mechanics and footwork become second nature to your body. They become like a language your body knows, ready to turn chaos into smooth, easy plays. Not only will learning these skills help you catch, but they will also make you feel better about your confidence. You'll know you can handle anything the game throws when you step onto the field. You'll go from being a fan in centerfield to being the undisputed outfield master.

Developing a strong

"And accurate arm."

The massive green space in the centerfield can be friends and enemies. It lets you show off your speed and range, but your arm has to be as strong as a gun. Imagine a deep fly ball going over the warning track and a runner on third base being brave enough to tag him. Your arm links defense and offense, turning a possible run into an exciting out. It would help if you had more than strength to build a solid and effective arm. You also need to be able to control and aim your movements. To become the director of a leather symphony, you must plan perfect throws from the outfield's depths. Understanding how to throw is the first step to building a solid arm. It's a dance between your legs, core, and upper body. Each part is vital for making force and moving that power to the ball. Starting with your legs, throw something. The initial motion comes from a strong push off the back leg. This momentum moves up your core, working your chest and giving you a stable base for throwing. The last part of the move is your upper body. Your shoulder and arm work like a whip, releasing all that energy with a strong wrist snap. To get better at throwing, you need to build up your strength. Your best bet is to do weight training, but it needs to be specific and aimed. Do routines that work on your core, shoulders, triceps, and back to improve the muscles you use when you throw. Also, don't forget about your legs. Strong legs are what make your throwing move possible. Work out with weights to build the engine that makes your throws possible. But being strong isn't enough on its own. It is just as important to be accurate. Think about how throwing a laser beam differs from throwing a shaky frisbee. That's the difference between a sharp throw that goes through the infield and a wild one that goes over the head of the catcher. This is where throwing techniques and doing it repeatedly come in handy. You must ensure your move is smooth and steady to get accurate throws. You should be able to control every throw and make sure the ball goes in a straight line with a good follow-through. Proper mechanics become more automatic the more you practice them, giving you a throwing motion you can depend on no matter what. Now it's time to talk about the tools of the trade: your throwing program. Here are some drills that will help you get more robust and more accurate:

Long Toss: In this traditional drill, you throw the ball to a partner farther and farther away. Start with a short distance and slowly make it longer as your arm strength grows. This strengthens you and shows you how to control the ball over longer distances.

Drills with weighted balls: Using a ball that is a little heavier than a regular baseball increases resistance, which makes your muscles work harder. When you switch back to a regular ball, this extra work gives you more throwing power.

Plyometrics: Explosive movements, like plyometric workouts, train your muscles to strengthen quickly. You can improve your throwing power by jumping throws, in which you jump a little before throwing.

In all drills, it's imperative to use the proper form. When throwing, it's better to have good form and less power than to give up form for strength. Breaking a bad habit you picked up as a child can be challenging.

You can do things besides drills to make your arm strong and effective.

Dynamic Stretching: It's essential to warm up your arm before throwing it to keep it from getting hurt. When you do dynamic stretches like shoulder shrugs and arm circles, your muscles get ready for the stress of throwing.

The proper distance to throw: don't go too far! If you throw too much too soon, your arms could tire and hurt. Start your throwing workouts slowly and build up the volume and length of your sessions over time. Pay attention to your body and rest when you need to.

Dedication to the Long Term: Building a solid arm takes time and hard work. Do not expect effects right away. Keep things the same. If you follow your throwing plan and practice daily, you'll get better over time.

Building a solid and effective arm takes more than just throwing harder. It would help if you believed in yourself. It makes you feel better about yourself on the pitch as your throws get more robust and accurate. You'll be able to stop runners at the plate quickly, make those saves in deep center that look impossible, and prevent the other team's offense. For centerfielders, a strong arm is a badge of honor that shows how dedicated they are to their job and how well they know the outfield. Prepare your glove and ball, fire up your inner gun, and become the undisputed king of the deep!

CHAPTER 2

SPEED, RANGE, AND INSTINCTS

Exercises to increase your speed

"And agility."

You can find a centerfield, a vast green area offering freedom and obstacles. It would help if you were fast like a lion and quick like a gazelle to own this land. Imagine a blazing line drive hurtling towards the gap and a baserunner rounding third with a sly grin on their face. You use your speed and agility as tools to block that hit and change the course of the game. How do you find this secret talent and become a blur on the pitch? The answer is an exercise plan focusing on making you faster and more reactive.

Speed: The Need for Need for Speed

Let's look at speed. Running across the pitch is made possible by your raw power, which lets you catch fly balls and stop-line drives before they reach the gap. This basic drill includes short bursts of movement at almost maximum effort. To warm up your muscles, jog slowly for a few minutes. Then, go to a flat, open place and run fast for 20 to 30 meters. Ensure you keep the correct form, including a strong arm swing, a high knee drive, and a vital leg extension. Jog slowly for about the same distance after each run to recover. Do this six to eight times. The hills are like natural resistance coaches for you. Find a slight slope and run as fast as you can up it. Hill runs make your legs more substantial and more explosive, which helps you go faster on flat ground. Remember to keep the proper form even when you're working hard. Start with shorter lengths and slowly raise the angle as your fitness level rises. In baseball, you don't just start from scratch. There are many times when you need to move quickly and run after the ball is hit. Flying starts to act out these situations. Place the cones 10 metres apart. Begin by running towards the cones. As you get close to them, go into a full sprint. This teaches your body to respond quickly and speed up.

Agility: The Art of Making Your Way Through the Game

It's not enough to just be fast. Athletes need to be able to change direction quickly and effectively. You can use this skill to handle unexpected scenarios, catch fly balls traveling in strange directions, and make diving catches that amaze everyone. To improve your agility, use a ladder. You can do a lot of drills with these simple tools that test your balance and footwork. Side shuffles, in-and-out steps, and single-leg hops are some drills you can try. Keep your center of gravity low and focus on making quick, accurate moves. Cones are a valuable tool for teaching in many ways. Form a pattern with cones in a square, triangle, or star shape. Run through the design and turn around each cone as quickly as possible. This tests your ability to respond and change your footwork while keeping up your speed. You don't need any tools for this drill. Pair up and stand opposite each other. Your partner will do different moves, like backpedals, jumps, and shuffles. It's your job to move precisely like them quickly and correctly. This works on your reaction time and makes it easier to handle things as they change.

How Speed and Agility Work Together

Speed and quickness aren't two separate things; they go together. They're like two sides of the same coin. Speed gets you where you need to go fast, and agility helps you get around in a highly complex game. Line up four cones in a square shape, leaving about 10 meters between each one. Run as fast as possible to the first cone, touch it, and slowly walk back to the starting place. Quickly run to the second cone, feel it, and slowly return to the starting spot. Keep going like this, switching between runs, backpedals, and shuffles. This drill is like playing centerfield because you must quickly change directions while keeping up high energy.

When you run with resistance bands, your muscles must work harder to keep up. Attach one end of a tension band to something that won't move and wrap it around your waist. Do your routine sprint drills, but this time, add some pressure. This makes you more powerful, so you can move faster and hit harder on the pitch. Before you work out, you should always do active stretches to warm up your muscles. Also, to avoid injuries, cool down with static stretches later. Do not push yourself too quickly. Gradually make your workouts harder and longer as your fitness level rises. Pay attention to your body and rest when you need to avoid getting hurt from overtraining. During practice, it's easy to give up form for speed. But this could cause bad habits and harm in the future. Use the proper form during your workouts, even when pushing yourself. Don't get stuck in a rut; try new things! Your workouts should include a range of drills to keep things exciting and give your body new challenges. Working out shouldn't feel like work. You should add drills that you enjoy to your practice. To keep things interesting, play music, work out with a friend, or make your workouts competitive.

With these drills, hard work, and the right attitude, you can find your hidden strengths and become unrecognizable. You'll be able to run after any fly ball and move quickly enough to handle the tricky play in centerfield. Keep in mind that speed and quickness are helpful, but they're not the only thing that matters. If you combine them with good fielding skills, a strong arm, and a love for the game, you'll be a true centerfield force that commands the vast stretch of green.

Reading the ball

"And taking efficient routes to the ball."

In the centerfield, a massive spread of green seems to go on forever. It's like a painting where the plays are a symphony of motion. But in the middle of this peace, a hitter hits the ball hard, breaking the silence. When the ball goes off, it makes a white cloud in the blue sky. Your heart beats faster, and energy flows through your body. Now is your chance. Reading the ball and finding the best way to make the catch are two skills that are very important for this play to work. Reading the ball isn't about figuring out secret messages; it's about getting the hang of the game's language. To guess where that white dot will land, look at the batter's swing, the ball's path, and other outside factors. Imagine a detective putting together signs like the batter's stance, the count, and the direction of the wind to figure out where the ball went.

The Art of Observation: Figuring Out What the Hitter's Clues Mean

Seeing the batter is the first thing you need to do to read the ball. How a batter stands can tell you a lot about what they plan to do. A tight stance usually means that the batter wants to pull the ball to the right (for righties) or left (for lefties) side. People who hit with an open stance wish to drive the ball the other way or hit for power to deep center. If a batter swings hard and the bat goes straight down, they are likelier to hit a line drive. They might fly the ball if they swing slowly and the bat rises. Keeping an eye on the bat path can help you guess the ball's initial launch position. Skilled players can even read a batter's body language without realizing it. If the batter moves their weight to one side, it can show where they want to hit the ball.

Looking at the Ball's Path: Following the Clues

When the ball leaves the bat, you focus on where it's going. The ball will go farther if it leaves the bat faster. You must take a quick first step and go straight for a fast line drive, but you can take your time for a slower fly ball. The ball's spin can change the way it flies. A backspin serves to push the ball down a bit, while a topspin can make it rise a bit before it starts to fall. If you know about spin, you can guess where the ball will rise and how it will fall. This sneaky factor can change the path of the ball by a lot. A strong wind from left field can push a fly ball further to right field and vice versa. Always check the direction of the wind and change your plan as needed.

Taking the Quick Way: Putting the Pieces Together

Once you have all the information you need, it's time to plan how to get to the catch. This is all about efficiency. You don't want to chase the ball around and around or take steps that aren't necessary. The first thing you do is crucial. Look at the angle of launch at the start and the expected path. It would help to fly straight at the ball when you hit a line drive. For a fly ball, you should come at it from an angle to get under it as it falls. You must backpedal quickly with small, controlled steps to track fly balls. Watch the ball and change your speed and direction to stay under it. It would help if you clarified to everyone that another player has a better chance at the ball. Communication keeps things clear and makes sure the catch goes smoothly. Reading the ball and finding the best routes can be worked on. Do drills like games, like having a person hit fly balls at different speeds and angles, or do drills like games where the wind is against you.

Beyond the Basics: More Advanced Strategies

Skilled players can guess where the ball will land based on the number of outs, the men on base, and the count. If you can guess where the ball is going, you can get a head start and progress faster. There are often deep walls in the centerfield. When you know the exact size of your area, you can play balls hit towards the wall better. If you jump at the right time against the wall, you might catch a fly ball that would have been a home run. Skilled centerfielders can sometimes use little lies to their advantage. They can trick baserunners into tagging up at third by taking a slightly deeper route at first for a fly ball. Then, they can quickly cut back towards the infield and catch the ball before it hits.

How to Get Good at It: Why Reading and Routing Are Beneficial

Reading the ball and taking innovative routes isn't just about making excellent catches; it's also about stopping runs and making the most of your defensive effort. It helps your team win whenever you get someone in centerfield or stop a play. There is no better feeling than hitting the ball perfectly and having it drop in your glove. It shows how hard you've worked, how well you know the game, and how well you can handle the considerable field in the centerfield.

A lot of work goes into becoming a great ball reader. Wait your turn, believe your gut, and keep improving your skills. Pretty soon, you'll look forward to the ball's dance, moving through the outfield gracefully and quickly and becoming a formidable defense force. There will be no more mysteries with high-fly balls. Instead, each will be a chance to show off your skills and become the best in the outfield.

Anticipating plays

"And covering maximum ground."

Imagine that there are two outs, the bases are complete, and a lot of stress is in the air. When the batter hits a line drive, you're already there with your hand outstretched, making a routine catch. How? The answer is anticipation, which is the secret tool of centerfielders because it lets them cover as much ground as possible and turn bad situations into defensive gems. When anticipating, you're not just going with your gut; you're making an intelligent guess based on how well you know the game. It's like being a great chess master who can see several moves ahead and plan your move based on what your opponent (the hitter) will do next. Each pitch has a story to tell. Pay close attention to the count. The batter may try to hit the ball far away if it's 3-2 with a runner on second. Look at how many outs there are. A fly ball could lead to an out at any base if there are two outs. You can guess what might happen next better if you know more about what is happening. Learn how to read people's bodies. Someone who hits with their stance tight and upper body coiled is probably going for a pull hit. If a batter moves their weight to the right field, they might try to hit the ball the other way. These small clues can help you determine what the batter is attempting to do.

Each pitcher has a unique pitch that they use. Make friends with your players and learn what they're good and bad at. You can plan for slower ground balls or pop-ups if you know that your pitcher throws a lot of breaking balls that get hit poorly. Put yourself in the place of the baserunner. If a runner is on first, a fastball could be used to try to steal second. If there are two outs and the runner is on second, they might take a chance on a fly ball, so move closer to the infield to stop them at third.

Putting Your Anticipation to Use

Now that you know how to build interest, it's time to use what you've learned. Plan where you will be before each pitch based on the situation, the count, and the batter's habits. This could mean playing a little deeper in case of a fly ball with two outs or leaning a little more to the pull side if that's how the batter usually hits. It's essential to have a good jump off the pitch. As the pitcher throws, try to guess what kind of pitch it will be and act accordingly. If the pitch is fast, you might need to jump faster; if it's breaking, you might need to jump a little later. You can get a head start on the ball if you master this jump. That angle is on your side: Run in circles sometimes. Get the most out of angles. If the fly ball is hit toward the gaps, play at an angle that lets you see the ball better while covering more ground.

How to Become a Master of the Outfield

You go from being a reactive player to being proactive when you can predict what will happen, read the ball, and find the best routes. You are now in charge of the defense in the fields and have to guess what the other team will do next. Every play is a chance to show how smart, spontaneous, and able to cover as much ground as possible you are.

Being able to anticipate things gets better with practice. You'll learn how to avoid problems and understand the rules of a game better the more you play it. Soon, you'll be a pro at playing outfield. Every play you make will amaze the other team's batters and make your team cheer.

CHAPTER 3

HITTING AND OFFENSIVE STRATEGY

A consistent swing

"And approach at the plate."

When you step into the batter's box, the bat hitting the bat and the pitcher looking you down is exciting and scary. As a centerfielder, your defense is essential, but don't forget how well you score. Here's where having a steady swing and a clear plan at the plate can help you.

The Art of the Swing

Imagine a sculptor working very carefully on a beauty. That is what a good swing is all about: it's like a well-oiled machine where every move fits together perfectly. Strong foundations are the first step to a good swing. Pay attention to your balance, grip, and weight distribution. Stay balanced by bending your knees, keeping your core tight, and holding the bat quickly in your hands. These basics give you a strong base for making power and controlling the bat. A great hitter always has a rhythm and smooth moves before the swing. This could be done with a bat wag or a slight leg kick. Try different things until you find what works best for you and lets you time the pitcher's delivery. If your rhythm is consistent, your swing mechanics will also be constant. It would help if you built muscle memory to get a steady swing.

Spend time on hitting skills like tee work, soft toss, and batting practice, and ensure every swing is done correctly. Making a smooth, strong swing gets easier the more you do it.

What Approach Can Do for You

A steady swing is essential, but it's not the only thing that matters. The difference between good and great hitters is having a precise method at the plate or a game plan that you stick to. Are you a contact hitter who waits for the right pitch or a power hitter who loves fastballs? It is imperative to know your skills and weaknesses. Each pitcher has a tale to share. Watch their warm-up pitches, figure out what they usually say, and try to guess what they'll say next. Are they a bowler who throws both fastballs and breaking balls? Or a curveball expert who throws a heater once in a while? You can change your method better if you know more about the pitcher. This is the best way to hit. Don't hit everything with your swing. Pay attention to pitches in your strike zone that you can hit hard. More good at-bats and a better batting average come from being disciplined. It's essential to change your strategy depending on the game. Putting runners on base might call for a substitute bunt. If you are down two runs and have two outs, it might be best to go for the home run.

Getting in Charge of the Plate

Having a straightforward approach and a consistent swing will change you from a passive hitter to an active player in the fight at the plate. The pitcher must throw strikes you can handle because you set the rules. Being sure of your swing and having a clear plan for how to hit the ball gives you confidence. When you walk up to bat, you have a clear head and are ready to hit any ball the pitcher throws. You can consistently hit the ball if you have a smooth swing and follow a strict plan. Putting the ball in play pushes the defense to make plays and gives your team chances to score, even if not every hit is a home run. It isn't perfect for pitchers when batters are calm and pick and choose. Making the pitcher throw strikes more often by fouling off pitches outside the strike zone repeatedly wears them down and improves your chances of getting hit when you try.

Getting your swing and technique at the plate takes time and hard work to be consistent. But the benefits are enormous. You become a more helpful player because you can help on defense and offense. Soon, you'll feel calm and in control when you walk into the batter's box. You'll be ready to release your swing and become a fierce force at the plate.

Utilizing your speed in bunting

"And hit-and-run situations."

Picture yourself as a centerfielder. You're a blur on the field, and your legs move like lightning. You're fast, but you can use it as a tool at the plate, too, not just to catch fly balls. You can show off your speed and complicate things for the other team's defense when you're bunting or hit-and-run. Here's how to use your edge and get good at these strategic moves.

Bunting: More Than Just a Plea

Bunting is often seen as a way to give up something essential to make a smart move forward. But it can be a potent attacking tool for a quick centerfielder. The batter hits a softball down the third-base line with this bunt. The third baseman has to catch the ball and throw it to first. This is where your speed shines. Move quickly towards the pitcher and bunt the ball down the third-base line as the pitcher throws. Run as fast as you can down the first-base line to force the defense to make a quick, accurate throw. Even if you get thrown out, you can still make things more complicated for the defense, which could lead to a bad throw or a chance for a partner to move forward. For this bunt, you hit the ball down the first-base line, which makes the first baseman catch it and throw it to first. Here, too, your speed is critical. Like with the drag bunt, take a small step toward the pitcher and bunt the ball around the line. Don't run straight towards first base, though. Instead, run with a slight angle toward the pitcher's mound. The first baseman's standard throwing path is blocked by this angle, which can lead to some confusion and a hasty or incorrect throw. A sudden but can be very useful sometimes because it throws the defense off guard. This move works best when the pitcher doesn't expect it, like when the count is 3-0 and a swing is more possible. In this case, you keep your hitting position the same, but at the last second, you change your bat path slightly to bunt the ball. Because you're fast, you might be able to get to first base before the defense does, which would give your team a chance to score.

The hit-and-run game is a speedster's dream.

You need to be quick and able to talk to your teammates to make the hit-and-run work. The batter and the player on first base agree on a hit-and-run play before the pitch. The runner has a big lead off of first base and is ready to steal on the first pitch. You are in centerfield, and your job is to talk to the runner and the other players in the infield. You should be aware and ready to act quickly. The runner on first base runs to second as the thrower throws. Your part is vital here. Because you're fast, you can get to the ball before the player does if they hit it, and it goes into play, especially on the right side of the field. The defense is under a lot of stress because of this. The player who would normally throw to second to get the runner out has to choose between throwing you out at first and trying to get the runner out at second. This gives the runner a critical split second of hesitation, which could let them safely get to second base.

The Art of Lying and Talking to People

Using your speed in bunting and hit-and-run situations takes more than being fast. If the runner on first base fakes a steal, it can sometimes be enough to throw off the defense. If the batter gets a big lead and looks like they'll steal on the first pitch, even if they don't, it can make the defense pause, leading to a hit-and-run later in the at-bat. Talking is essential. Before the pitch, ensure everyone agrees on whether the hit-and-run should happen. To start the game, a simple hand signal or a set phrase can be used to avoid misunderstanding.

Practice Makes Perfect: Getting Good at It

Work on your bunting with a coach or a partner. Pay attention to bunting the ball correctly and softly in different directions. Practice hitting someone and then running away with your friends. Someone else plays first base while the batter hits off of a tee or throws a coach's fungo. As the fielder, practice your response time by running after hitting the ball. Bunting and hit-and-run should be a part of scrimmages and practice games. In this way, you can feel the stress and chaos of a real game and improve your skills in a more realistic setting.

One of the benefits of speed is that it makes you stronger.

You can be a real force at the plate if you know how to use your speed well in bunting and hit-and-run situations. The other defense has no idea what will happen to you. They have to change their plan for every pitch because they don't know if you'll swing or slide. The constant change keeps them on their toes and gives your team chances to get ahead. Bunting and hit-and-run situations can be very useful for moving runners over and making chances to score. A bunt or hit-and-run that goes well can change the game's outcome. Your speed throws off the defense's flow. They have to decide quickly and throw the ball accurately, which can cause mistakes and stolen bases. The defense has to play perfectly to get you out because you become a constant threat.

Beyond Speed: Everything You Need

Being fast is helpful, but it's not the most important thing. Learning how to bounce will help you consistently place and control the ball. You should be able to softly bunt the ball in different ways so that the defense doesn't know what to do. It's important to know what's going on in the game. To understand when to bunt, hit-and-run, or go for the home run, you need to know the score, the number of outs, and the men on base. An excellent ability to run bases is required in a hit-and-run to work. The person on first base needs to get a good head start, guess what the pitcher will do, and make a quick, decisive break for second base.

When you combine your lightning-fast speed with these other skills, you become a full offensive force that makes it impossible for pitchers and defenses to stop you. If you slide the ball in the right place, it will start a rally. It will mess up the defense if you hit and run at the right time. Speed is a tool. When you play baseball, how you use it makes you a real threat.

Base running techniques

"And stealing bases."

As a centerfielder, you have to do more than patrol the vast green area and make excellent saves. It's about being a threat on the base paths and a constant pain for the other team. This is where learning to steal and run bases becomes your secret tool. You go from being good at defense to being great at offense, which puts pressure on the defense and gives your team chances to score.

What You Need to Know About Base Running: How to Run Like a Blur

Before we learn how to steal bases, let's ensure we have the basics: how to run the bases correctly. Let's talk about leads. A good lead enables you to get to the next base ahead of the catcher's throw without getting caught. As a centerfielder, you won't likely take as much of a lead on first base as a second baseman or someone who steals bases. But work on being bold while still being in control, reading the pitcher's delivery, and guessing the next play. Other leads come into play after the ball is hit. You have to read the ball off the bat and take calculated chances to get an extra base. If the ball is hit far out in left field, for example, you might take a big secondary lead from first base and try to tag up and score on a double. Sliding backward lets you get to the base safely and might stop the fielder from throwing. Learn how to do it right by bending your knees, keeping your head down, and stretching your leg out to touch the base. It takes a lot of skill to be good at base running. It is imperative to know what is happening, like the score, the number of outs, and who is on base. Some choices make a difference between good and great base runners. For example, great base runners know when to stop at a base to avoid a double play and when to take an extra base on a wild pitch.

The Thrill of the Steal: What the Art Means

Let's talk about taking bases, which is the hardest thing for base runners to do and the bravest thing they can do. Your boss gives you the green light, which means you can try to steal the ball. This choice is made by looking at the pitcher's habits (for example, does he throw slowly to first?), the catcher's arm strength, and the game's score. It's essential to have a decisive jump off the ball. Read the pitcher's delivery and try to guess when the ball will be released. If you can jump well, you can get a big head start on getting to second base. It's essential to get good at the slide move when taking bases. Before the tag is put on, you must get to the base safely. You can steal a base if you slide well enough to mess up the throw and make the other player make a mistake. An excellent fake steal can work just as well as a real one sometimes. If you have a big lead and look like you'll steal on the first pitch, it can throw off the pitcher and catcher. Later in the at-bat, this could make it possible for someone to steal home.

The Mental Game: How to Read the Pitcher and Trick the Defence

It's not just about being strong; stealing bases is also a mental fight. Watch how the pitcher throws the ball. Does he throw slowly to first base, which could give you more time to steal? Does he often hesitate, which gives you a chance to steal for free? How you try to steal is better planned if you know more about the player. Learn how to read signs from the thrower to the catcher. This can help you figure out whether the pitcher will throw a heater or a breaking ball, which can change how you jump and steal. Remember that stealing signs is against the rules in Major League Baseball, but paying attention to the catcher's body language and other subtle hints can still help you. As you steal, try to guess what the catcher will throw. Where do you think it will go? Is the catcher known for having a solid or weak arm? Because you know what's coming, you can change your slide and maybe escape a tag.

"The Art of the Steal: More Than Just Running the Bases"

This is clear-cut. Being fast gives you a significant edge when beating the throw to second base. Be brave, and don't be afraid to take chances. Base thieves who are good at what they do aren't scared to go for it, so the defense has to make a great play to get them out. But don't mix up being bold with being careless. Think about what's happening and take risks with a good chance of paying off. You can understand how the game works and make intelligent choices on the base paths if you have a good baseball IQ. To be a good base stealer, you need to know when to steal when to hold at a base to draw a throw, and when to take an extra base on a wild pitch. It takes more than one person to steal bases. Talk to your team members, especially the batter. If you want to steal, the hitter might have to shorten their swing on a hit-and-run play or fake a bunt to get the throw first, which gives you more time to steal.

As a stolen base's reward, you can put pressure on the defense.

A good stolen base can change the whole course of a game. If you steal second base, you put yourself in a situation to score. Now, a single or a base hit by a partner can send you home, making it possible for other players to score and forcing the defense to change how they play. It's hard for the pitcher to keep up when a base is taken. Now, he has to worry about the man on second, which could make it harder for him to concentrate and choose which pitch to throw. To put pressure on the defense, every base that is taken makes the defense work harder. A pitch must hit you and then be caught by a catcher or middle infielder. This stress can make people make mistakes, which gives your team a chance to score.

Getting Good at Something: Practice Makes Perfect

Get better at quickly taking leads, rounding bases, and sliding correctly. You can also get faster and more athletic by doing running runs and agility drills. Practice with your friends by acting out different game situations. Run through situations where you must steal bases, take second leads, and decide how to run the bases based on the play. Watch major league baseball games to see how good base stealers do their job. Look at their strategies, how they make decisions, and how they plan plays.

You become a more helpful player for your team when you learn how to run the bases well and become a threat on the base paths. You're not just a defensive expert watching over the outfield; you're also a constant offensive weapon that makes it hard for the defense to play and creates chances to score. Base thieves who are physically strong, mentally sharp, and ready to take calculated risks are the best. Now that you have your shoes on work on your lead and get ready to steal your way to becoming a top baseball player.

CHAPTER 4

THE LEADER OF THE OUTFIELD

Communicating effectively

"With fellow outfielders and infielders."

Think about this: a line drive flies off the bat and into the space between the outfielders. Fear sets in. Who wants it? Who is there to back up who? It's a mess, and the ball hits the ground for a base hit. This situation shows how important it is for baseball players, especially outfielders and infielders, to talk to each other. When everyone on defense is on the same page, things that could go badly can turn into great plays. Here's how to improve your speaking skills so that you can lead your team to a smooth and confident defense.

The Foundation: Getting Ready Before the Game

Before the first ball is even thrown, good communication starts. Talk to your outfielders and infielders about how you plan to defend each batter before the game. Will you play a shift to the pull side for a right-handed batter? Are the infielders going farther out to get ground balls? Everyone is ready to handle any hit ball if they can talk to each other. Make a list of verbal or hand signs that will be used to show who is taking the fly ball. This keeps things clear and ensures everyone knows who controls the catch. Some common signs are pointing your glove at the ball, shouting, "I got it!" or saying a set phrase like "mine" or "yours." Talk about back-up plans in case there are misunderstandings or unplanned events. Agree on who will help the other outfielder if the ball goes far into the gap. So, even if the first call is missed, someone will always be ready to make the play.

The Game Starts: Making the Shots

As the game goes on, communicating is even more critical. Watch the ball as it leaves the bat to see where it's going. Use your pre-set signal to call for it if it's safely in your zone. Be brave and make a loud, clear call. That way, everyone will know you have it. When a fly ball lands in the space between two outfielders, they must talk to each other. The outfielder closest to the ball should call for it right away, and the other outfielder should accept the call and be ready to step in if something goes wrong. Line drives need quick responses and clear communication. If someone hits a line drive at another outfielder, a quick "on you!" or direction calls like "left!" or "right!" can keep the play from getting shaky. If there is an infield fly rule, the player closest to the ball should immediately call it out loud and clear. This lets the infielders and base runners know what's happening, avoiding misunderstanding and possible double plays.

"More Than Calls: Active Communication"

Calls aren't the only way to communicate clearly. Talk to your fellow outfielders and infielders all the time, even when nothing is happening right now. Phrases like "heads up" or "looking good" can help everyone stay on task and aware. Don't forget how powerful body language can be. You can effectively communicate by pointing to a spot where a ground ball might go or subtly waving your glove to show a possible cut-off. People make mistakes. After a mistake, cheer on and help your friends. A simple "good hustle" or "next time" can boost confidence and keep the team from getting distracted by bad news.

Working with the infield while respecting roles

Outfielders don't just talk to each other when they talk. Infielders have different ways of speaking to each other. For cut-offs, exchanges, and double plays, learn their signs. Knowing them well lets you guess what they'll need and give it to them. When it comes to calls, you should listen to the infielder when they call for a fly ball in their zone, even if it looks like it could be caught from the outfield. They might be able to see the ball better or from a better angle. Believe in your friends and put a smooth catch ahead of an individual effort. It would help if you weren't afraid to start talking to the infield. If you see a possible double play or a base runner trying to get away, let the infield know what you see so they can make the best play.

The Advantages of Smooth Communication: A Defence

Learning to talk to people can turn your team's defense from a disorganized mess into a well-oiled machine. Not talking to each other clearly can cause mistakes and lost chances. Errors happen less often when everyone is on the same page and knows who is taking the ball and helping each other. Being able to communicate clearly on the pitch builds trust. Feeling confident and at ease is easier when your friends have your back, and everyone works together. A great defensive play can turn the game's tide in your favor. The other team will lose motivation if you explain your catch well, make a perfect cut-off, or turn a double play smoothly.

Beyond the Field: Talking to each other makes a team.

Good communication between players builds trust and a sense of belonging. You become a true team when you learn to depend on each other. If you can talk to your friends clearly, you can cheer them on after an excellent or foul play. This positive atmosphere helps build a mindset of teamwork. Talking to each other lets you deal with possible issues on the pitch quickly and effectively. You can talk about changes and adapt as the game goes on if a specific plan isn't working.

Always getting better: a lifelong journey.

Communication is a skill that needs to be worked on and improved constantly. Watch footage of old games and look at how communication broke down. Find ways you can do better and talk about them with your friends. Setting up situations that need clear communication during practice, like fly balls in the gap or line drives to another outfielder, are called simulations. For example, this lets you work on your talking skills in a safe setting. Pay attention to your peers' calls and body language as you listen. This enables you to respond appropriately and guess what they need.

A good baseball defense depends on people being able to talk to each other. You become more than just a player when you learn how to speak to your fellow outfielders and infielders clearly and concisely. You become a leader, like an orchestra director, leading the defense to a perfect performance. When everyone on the pitch speaks with one voice, the team is more potent and can stop opponents, make scoring chances, and eventually win. Get better at talking to each other, get to know your friends well, and show how powerful a well-coordinated defense can be on the baseball field.

Taking charge of fly balls

"And pop-ups."

You're the outfield general as a centerfielder, watching over a massive area of green. You are in charge of more than just the outfield walls, though. You are also in charge of the air above them, especially for fly balls and pop-ups. Here's how to go from being a passive observer to a fearless leader who takes charge of fly balls and pop-ups and turns possible defense mistakes into stunning plays.

Knowing Your Turf: Understanding Where Fly Balls Go

Let's set up your name first before we take charge. Outfielders who play centerfield tend to play deeper than corner fielders. This lets you cover more ground and respond to line shots that might cut into the gaps. Set clear rules for how to talk to your corner outfielders. Talk about the "zones" for fly balls based on the pitcher and how they usually hit the ball before each pitch. This keeps things clear and ensures everyone knows whose job to catch the ball is. Figure out how to read the batter's swing and habits. Does the hitter often hit the ball to right field? There are a lot of fly balls. This information lets you plan your move before the pitch is even thrown.

Taking Charge: From Responding to Controlling Things Before They Happen

Let's talk about how to handle fly balls and pop-ups now. Please don't wait until the ball is almost before you ask for it. Make a loud, clear call when you see the ball leave the bat and know it's in your zone. This keeps things clear and lets your friends help you if you need it. Make your calls sound like you're sure of yourself. A strong "I got it!" or a clear direction call like "mine!" makes it clear that you own the play and stops you from hesitating. Once you call for the ball, you can only think about it. Please pay close attention to its path and change your position and movement as needed. Don't pay attention to the batter or the men on base.

Getting Good at the Basics: Tracking and Catching

It's not enough to call for the ball to be in charge. First, use your side vision to keep an eye on the ball. As it gets closer, look it straight in the eyes. This will help you get a better idea of its distance and path. Learn how to backpedal quickly for footwork while keeping your eyes on the ball. You can stay grounded and change your position by taking small, controlled steps. Keep your glove open and up, giving the ball a place to go. As you get closer to the catch point, move your glove to line up with the ball's path. Don't overthink about the catch. Focus on taking a soft, controlled grab and squeezing the ball hard once you have it.

Keeping Your Cool: How to Handle the Unexpected

Even the most skilled centerfielder will have to deal with things they didn't expect. It can be hard to play fly ball when the sun is in your eyes. Use your hand to protect your eyes and your side vision to follow the ball. In these cases, talking to your teammates is even more critical. Wind can change the path of a fly ball in a big way. Figure out how the wind is blowing and move your position to match. Plan for the ball to move a certain way and change your path to meet it. Talking to and being aware of your teammates is essential to avoid crashes. If a fly ball lands between you and another player, make sure there are clear calls first and change your routes to avoid a possible collision in the air.

The mental game is part of "Beyond the Fundamentals."

Taking charge of fly balls and pop-ups takes more than physical skill. Trust that you can make the play. Being sure of yourself leads to clear decisions and effortless performance. Stay laser-focused the whole at-bat. It's important not to let other things confuse you. Don't think about catches you missed all the time. Get over it, learn from it, and move on to the next play.

Setting a good example for your team members

It's not enough to catch the ball to be in charge. When you play centerfield, you take charge of the field. Use good communication to boost your friends' spirits even when you're not calling for the ball. A simple "heads up" or "looking good" can make them feel better about themselves and help them stay on task. When fly balls are hit near the edges of your area, you should always be ready to back up your corner outfielders.

Working hard and talking to each other adds extra safety and avoids missing possible saves. No matter how big or small, celebrate every defensive out. Giving your friends a high-five or a quick shout-out encourages them to play better defense and builds team spirit.

When you take charge, you get more than catches.

It's not enough to make incredible saves to be in charge of fly balls and pop-ups. Clear communication and aggressive control cut down on misunderstandings and dropped fly balls, making the defense less likely to make mistakes. The team has more confidence when the centerfielder is sure of himself and takes charge. It makes you feel safe knowing someone is always ready to catch fly balls. A well-done fly ball catch or a diving grab can change the game's flow. It can make the other team lose motivation and boost your own.

A Promise to Excellence: Continuous Improvement

You must keep practicing and committing to get good at taking charge. Track fly balls while you bat during batting practice. Have your friends hit fly balls to different parts of the outfield. This will force you to change where you are and how you backpedal. Doing runs in various types of wind helps you learn how the wind changes the path of a fly ball. This lets you better guess how the ball will move and change where you are standing to match. Workouts that use visualization can be powerful. Imagine following fly balls, jumping to catch them, and leading your team on defense. This mental practice makes you feel better about yourself and helps you concentrate during games.

You go from being a passive observer to a natural outfield leader when you learn how to handle fly balls and pop-ups. You become a leader who makes your teammates believe in themselves and controls the defensive flow of the game. Taking charge isn't just about making fantastic saves; it's also about communicating, staying focused, and wanting to do the best. It would help if you got better, set a good example, and become the precise king of the fly zone, a player that can't be crossed off.

Setting an example

"With your work ethic and attitude."

There's more to being a good partner than hitting home runs or diving for balls. A real boss motivates their team not only with their skills but also with how hard they work and how they act. These are the unseen factors that shape the character of a team and, in the end, affect how well they do. Here are potent ways to lead your friends on and off the pitch.

The Grind Never Stops: Drawing Attention to an Unwavering Work Ethic

You don't have to be the most significant or flashiest player as a worker. It's about a quiet commitment to always getting better. Get to practice early and stay late to do extra work. It would help if you worked on improving your skills in every part of the game by doing fielding drills, hitting sessions, and weight training. Your friends are motivated to do better because of how committed you are. Don't avoid the complex parts of training. Do fitness drills even if they make you tired. Ensure your friends see how hard you work to improve, even when things get tough. A good boss always knows how to play the game. Look at replays, think about how you did, and constantly look for ways to improve. This desire to learn drives your teammates to stay interested and work hard at growing.

Outside the Field: Keeping a Positive Attitude

A good mood spreads like wildfire. It makes everyone on the team feel good and creates a welcoming space where everyone can do well. Bring your "A" game when it comes to being excited. Support your friends, enjoy their wins, and keep a positive attitude even when they lose. They stay inspired and focused during the whole game because of your energy. Be a partner who helps each other instead of someone who brings them down. Encourage players who are having a hard time, enjoy their wins, and build a sense of teamwork on and off the pitch. Everyone makes mistakes. When bad things happen, get back on your feet quickly, learn from them, and keep your head up. Your friends know how to deal with problems and keep a positive attitude from watching you.

The Ripple Effect: How What You Do Affects the Team

Your hard work and good mood aren't just happening by themselves. When you put hard work and happiness first, you help create a team culture that values commitment, growth, and helping each other. This strengthens the group, making everyone feel appreciated and driven to do their best. When you lead by example, people are more likely to be responsible for their work ethic and mood. People around you will be likelier to do their best if you put in extra effort and keep a happy attitude. People who work hard, help each other, and keep a good mood are more likely to succeed in the long run. A winner's mindset is built on your hard work and positive attitude.

"Setting a Good Example: It's Not About You"

Setting a good example isn't about getting attention for yourself or being praised. It involves making a good place where everyone can do well. There is a thin line between showing others how to do something and bragging. Your hard work and good mood should speak for themselves. Don't brag about what you've done; instead, focus on helping your teammates—things you do say louder than words. Don't just say you'll work hard and stay upbeat; show it by what you do daily. Show your friends how committed you are by always being dedicated and positive. Allow your teammates to give you input and talk to you. Listen to what they say if they think you could improve your mood or work ethic.

Work ethic and attitude are the things that make a team great that you can't see. You can help build a culture of dedication, support, and the pursuit of excellence on your team by setting the goal of constant growth, keeping a positive attitude, and leading by example. No matter your rank, authentic leadership is about getting people to be their best selves on and off the pitch. Do your best, have a good attitude, and put in the work. You'll be surprised at how much of an effect you can have on your team.

MENTAL TOUGHNESS AND FOCUS

Staying engaged

"And ready for every pitch."

A lot of things can happen in baseball. A game can go in any direction with just one bat swing. It would be best to be mentally sharp from the first pitch to the last to make the most of these chances. Here are some tips on staying interested and ready for every pitch, changing yourself from a bystander to an involved player.

Tuning Out the Noise: Getting Rid of Distractions

A baseball pitch can be noisy with the bat's crack, the crowd's roar, and the chatter on the bench. Set up a plan before the game that helps you get ready mentally. This could be done by doing deep breathing routines, visualizing, or listening to music that calms you down. Find something that helps you calm down before the first ball. Don't think about your mistakes or what might happen in the future. Focus on the pitch, the play, and the issue as you train your mind to be in the present. To stay interested, use outside signs. Pay attention to the catcher's mitt, watch the pitcher's movements, or listen to the rhythm of the pitcher's delivery. These outside cues can help you keep your mind on the game and keep you focused on the flow of it.

Keeping Up The Intensity: Avoiding Mental Lulls

Focusing your mind isn't always possible. Keeping up the energy throughout the whole game takes a lot of work. On the baseball pitch, each person has a specific job to do. Whether you're the batter, the fielder, or the runner on first, know your duties and think about how to perform them every time. It's fun to look forward to baseball games. Watch the pitcher's body language, guess what the baserunner will do, and picture what could happen. This active preparation keeps your mind busy and ready for anything that might occur. Talking badly to yourself can be hard on the mind. Could you change it to upbeat affirmations? Not "I can't get a hit," but "I'm focused and ready to attack this pitch."

Mental toughness means getting back up after a setback.

Everybody messes up sometimes. A bad swing or a mistake in the field can happen very quickly in baseball. Baseball is a game where you forget things quickly. Don't overthink about a play you missed. Get over it, learn from it, and move on to the next pitch. Dwelling on mistakes will only make you less effective in the present. Things can change quickly in the game. Be willing to change your plan if it's not working. This could mean changing how you hit the ball, play defense, or run the bases. A tough player can deal with problems and adapt to new situations. All the hard work you did when you practiced. Believe in your gut and what you've been taught. Do not let one setback make you lose faith.

The Power of Engagement: How It Can Change Your Game

Being focused makes you act more quickly. You'll be able to respond faster to a fastball, guess when a breaking pitch will come, and play defense with more confidence. When you play baseball, you have to make quick choices. When you focus, you can think clearly, quickly assess situations, and make the best choices on the field, whether at bat, basepaths, or outfield. Ensuring you're locked in and focused on the game makes you feel better about yourself. You feel like you're in charge of the game and have faith in your skills, which makes you perform better overall.

It's not easy to pay attention to every pitch, but it's an essential skill for any baseball player. You can go from being a passive player on the pitch to an active force by training your mind to focus, block out distractions, and be mentally tough. Remember that the game benefits those who can keep their mind on it, act quickly, and refuse to let go from the first pitch to the last. Accept the challenge, work on your mental game, and become the dedicated player your team wants you to be.

Handling the highs

"And lows of the game."

Baseball. It's a game of inches, moments, and clean, honest feeling. A single bat hit can send you flying, and a mistake on defense can make you feel like you swallowed a lead weight. One of the most important things about being a great player is not just how good they are but also how well they can handle the highs and lows of the game. Regardless of the score, here's how to handle the emotional ups and downs, keep calm, and become a better player.

Riding the Highs: How to Stay Grounded in Happiness

The tallest home run. That is a crucial catch. These times can make you feel like you can't be defeated. Rejoice when you win or make a big play. Feel what you're feeling, and let the cheers wash over you. Enjoy your success and the teamwork that made it possible for a moment. Do not stay high for too long. Please take a moment to recognize and enjoy it, and then return to the job. The game isn't over yet, and getting too comfortable can quickly cost you. You're not a superhero just because you have a great play. Keep your cool, remember your part in the team, and keep working hard for yourself and your teammates.

"Facing the Lows: How to Deal with Disappointment"

A strikeout looking and a fly ball that was dropped. Sometimes, these things feel like a punch in the gut. Please recognize the feeling and let it out. Don't hold your feelings inside. Allow yourself to feel the anger and sadness. It gets worse when you try to hide it. "Own Your Mistakes" means owning up to your mistakes. Look at what went wrong, learn from it, and use it as inspiration to do better next time. It would help if you had a short memory. Baseball is a game where you forget things quickly. Stay away from the mistake. Get over it, learn from it, and be ready for the next chance.

Mental Toughness: The Key to Managing Your Feelings

Before the game, picture yourself winning different kinds of games. This mental practice boosts your confidence and prepares you for good and bad results. Continue to talk positively to yourself. Negative thoughts about yourself can hurt you the most after you've made a mistake. Could you change it to upbeat affirmations? "I can make the next play" or "I'm still in this game" can change how you feel in a big way. Everyone needs a good way to get rid of their anger. Make it a habit to clear your mind after each game. It could be talking to a friend, listening to music, or walking.

The Ripple Effect on Emotional Leadership

You set the mood for the whole group when you stay calm after striking out or cheer for a teammate's win with absolute joy. A steady presence gives the team trust and helps them stay on task. We all have hard times sometimes. After a challenging play, be there for your team. Giving them a pat on the back or a word of support can help them feel better and keep them going. You help build a solid, focused team attitude by controlling your emotions and being there for your teammates. You can weather any storm and come out better as a group because you have a united spirit.

You have to think about baseball as well as move your body. By being aware of your feelings, building mental toughness, and being a good model for your teammates, you take control of your emotions instead of letting them control you. You learn to enjoy the good times and deal with the bad ones to become a player who can regularly help your team win. You'll get curve balls in the game, but how you handle them makes you a player. Step up to the plate, take a deep breath, and handle your feelings with the same skill you use to hit a ball or make a play. You can do this.

Building confidence

"And resilience."

Stick with it: baseball is a challenging game. Even the best players fail more often than they win in this sport. Conversely, that battle can help you build something powerful: unwavering confidence and toughness. Here's how to turn losses into opportunities, doubt into faith, and become a player who does well when things get tough.

Growing a growth mindset is part of "The Seeds of Confidence."

Confidence is like a muscle that must be worked out constantly. Don't avoid harsh conditions. See them as chances to get better and learn. A formidable opponent or a difficult pitch are ways to test your skills and improve your play. Results aren't the only thing that builds confidence. The reason for this is how hard you worked during training. Focus on getting better, learning the basics, and putting in the work you need to be successful. You can be proud of yourself even before you hit a home run. Honor every accomplishment, no matter how small. Getting a good swing or a good catch in practice are both wins that help you grow as a person.

Learning from Mistakes: How to Turn Setbacks into Stepping Stones

In baseball, mistakes are bound to happen. Don't be afraid to own up to your mistakes. Figure out what went wrong, take what you learned, and do your best not to repeat the same error. Look at how other players deal with losing. Watch how your more experienced coworkers deal with mistakes and use what they've learned to fuel their drive. Don't be afraid to ask coaches or coworkers for help. A helpful criticism can show you your weak spots and help you determine what to work on.

Getting mentally tough means making your inner strength stronger.

Picture yourself doing well in different scenarios. Picture yourself pulling off a challenging play, taking on a task, and dealing with stress. This mental practice makes you feel better about yourself and prepares you for anything the game throws at you. Use positive mantras to fight negative self-talk. Say, "I'm ready, I'm focused, and I can do this," instead of "I can't do this." Set a routine before the game that helps you concentrate and calm down. One way to do this is to do deep breathing routines, listen to soothing music, or picture yourself succeeding. Setting up a pattern gives you a sense of control and calms you down before a game.

Building Team Confidence: Putting Each Other First

Being confident and strong can spread to others. Reward your partners for their wins, no matter how small. When someone gives you a high-five after a good hit or words of support after a challenging play, it makes the team feel supported and boosts their confidence. Talk about how you overcame problems and failures in your own lives. This lets your friends learn from your problems and become stronger. Baseball is a team sport. You can win and lose at the same time. Focus on working together, supporting each other, and enjoying wins as a group.

Making yourself more confident and strong isn't always easy. You can go from being a player who breaks down under pressure to one who thrives on it by taking on challenges, learning from your mistakes, and making the team setting more supportive. When you work hard and are willing to learn, you gain confidence—being resilient means meeting problems head-on and coming out stronger on the other side. You can be an unstoppable force on the pitch, a player who makes your teammates and you feel strong and confident. Take a stand, and remember that the next task is just another chance to show your strength.

CHAPTER 6

GAME DAY AND BEYOND

Establishing a pre-game routine

Things can go wrong in baseball. The pitcher might throw you curve balls, the hitter might feel pressure, and even a few fly balls you didn't see coming. But you can be in charge if you do something before the game. Your own set of habits helps you concentrate, calm down, and feel ready to play when you get to the pitch.

Why Do You Need a Routine?

Your habit is like a warm-up for your body and mind. Fear before a game is real. A habit helps you deal with them by giving you a familiar pattern that makes you feel calm and enables you to concentrate. If you do the same things repeatedly, your mind will learn to switch into "game mode," which will help you focus on the job and block out other thoughts. A set pattern lets you feel in charge of your pre-game preparation. You feel confident because you know exactly what you must do to be ready. Your body works well with routine. A routine before a game helps your muscles prepare for action, improving your ability and coordination.

Putting together your pre-game routine

There is no one-size-fits-all practice that will work for everyone. Are you prone to stress? Do you find it hard to concentrate? First, figure out what your biggest pre-game problems are. Change your habit so that it meets these needs. Do not be scared to try new things. You could listen to music, picture yourself succeeding, stretch, or do some short meditation. Find out what helps you stay calm and focused. Stick to a plan once you find one that works! To get the rewards, you need to do it over and over. Repeating your process makes it better at getting your mind and body ready.

What Makes a Strong Routine

Light dynamic stretches, throwing drills, and batting practice are all great ways to warm up and prepare to play. Visualization is a vital tool. Picture yourself making great plays, hitting the ball perfectly, and being sure of yourself on the pitch. Deep breathing techniques can also help you calm down and concentrate better. Play upbeat music, watch inspiring videos, or talk to friends who make you feel good. Put yourself in situations that make you feel good to boost your confidence and prepare for the game. Eat a healthy, well-balanced meal during the game to keep you going. Stay away from big meals that might make you feel tired.

Outside of the Normal: Superstitions and All

Lucky socks, a particular gum flavor, or a sure way to wear their outfit are all important for many players. Even though they're unnecessary, these superstitions can make your practice feel more comfortable and good about yourself. But it's best to let go of a myth if it makes you anxious or slows you down.

Keeping Your Focus During the Game

The things you do before a game are just the start. Don't think about mistakes you've made or worry about what might happen. You should pay attention to the current pitch, the current play, and the current situation. Watch the pitcher's mechanics, look at the catcher's mitt, or listen to the pitcher's delivery beat. Outside cues can help you keep your mind on the game and keep you focused. Say good things to yourself instead of negative things. Not "I can't get a hit," but "I'm focused and ready to attack this pitch."

Creating a practice before a game is an investment in your performance. You can feel focused, confident, and ready to win on the diamond before every game if you take the time to make a set of rituals that work for you. Try new things, get into a groove, and hit the pitch with a clear head and a strong swing!

The opposing hitters

"And pitchers."

It's half the battle in baseball to know your opponent. You can get a significant edge on the pitch by learning about the hitting and pitching styles of the players you'll be up against. How to become a master at reading your opponents' minds:

Hitter Scouting: Turn your deck into a crime scene

Find out whether the hitter does better against right-handed or left-handed bowlers. This could change how you play or where you stand defensively. Are they sluggers crushing fastballs or a contact hitter sending the ball all over the field? This information helps you pick pitches and guess how a batter will hit. Does the batter have difficulty breaking balls, or do they love going after fastballs? Look at their past at-bats to see what pitches they did well and poorly against. In what part of the field does the batter usually hit the ball? Figuring out their "hot zones" helps you put your fielders in the best positions for defense.

Pitcher Scouting: Figuring Out What's Going on the Mound

What throws does the pitcher throw? Is it a heater, slider, curve ball, and change-up? Knowing their repertoire lets you guess what throws they'll make next and change how you will hit them. When the pitcher throws, do they like to paint the corners or hang out on the edges of the strike zone? Knowing where they want to hang out helps you narrow the zone and wait for your pitch. Is the pitcher a flamethrower with fastballs that hit too hard, or is they a control pitcher with perfect accuracy? If you know their style, you can change how you hit and how patient you are at the plate. Does the pitcher try to blow you away with fastballs or use off-speed pitches to get you out? If you know how they use two strikes, you can change your swing and maybe surprise them.

Go Beyond Stats: Watch the Game Play Out

Watch how the thrower throws and how the catcher reads the ball. Do you notice any clues that point to the next pitch? As the player throws more pitches, they may lose control or get out of position. Be ready to take advantage of any weaknesses that might exist. If you see something during the game, don't be afraid to change how you play. If the pitcher throws a new pitch, you should be ready to respond and change your swing to match.

You'll have a significant advantage over your opponent if you learn the game, figure out scouting reports, and watch how things go in games. Information is power. Use it to improve your game and take the pitch by storm.

Strategies for staying healthy

"And performing at your best."

You have to be mentally and physically strong to play baseball. How to make a winning plan that keeps you fit, sharp, and ready to take the field by storm:

How to Fuel Your Body: The Athlete's Diet

Eat for Performance: A healthy diet of fruits, veggies, and whole grains is essential. These give you long-lasting energy and the necessary nutrients to perform at your best.

Water is critical: You should always be near water. Stay hydrated all day to avoid getting tired, sharpen your mind, and make sure your muscles work right.

Pay attention to your body: Don't skip meals or overeat. Eat well-balanced meals regularly to keep your energy level steady and avoid getting nervous before a game.

Recovery After the Game: Eat a healthy meal or drink a protein shake to help your muscles repair and give your body more energy.

Getting Smarter: The Mental Game

Aim for 7-8 hours of sound sleep every night. Getting enough sleep helps you concentrate, respond quickly, and think overall. Baseball can be difficult. To deal with stress healthily, try yoga, meditation, or spending time in nature. Picture yourself winning different game situations. Picture yourself making great plays, hitting the ball perfectly, and being sure of yourself on the pitch. Say good things to yourself instead of negative things. Not "I can't get a hit," but "I'm focused and ready to attack this pitch."

Taking Care of Your Body: Keeping Your Body Safe

Getting stronger makes you more active and increases the power of your swing and the speed of your throws. Strength training should be a regular part of your practice. Stretching makes it easier to move and lowers your risk of getting hurt. Stretching every day will help you keep your body flexible. Do not push through pain. If you're not feeling well, take a break and rest. If you need to, see a doctor. Do not forget how important it is to warm up properly before practice or a game and cool down properly afterward. This gets your body ready for exercise and helps it heal.

If you follow these tips, you'll be well on your way to becoming a well-rounded player. Taking care of your mind and body is as important as working on your swing or getting better at throwing. Just be your best self on and off the pitch, and you'll do great!

Closing Thoughts

Baseball is a path where you always learn, change, and improve. This e-book should have given you the information and tools to feel confident on this trip. Don't forget that the most critical parts of the game are not inside the bases or the outer walls. It's about being committed, not giving up, and always believing in your abilities. Take on the challenges, learn from your mistakes, and enjoy your big or small wins. Before you go out on the pitch, take a deep breath and think about what you've learned here. Pay attention to the present, believe in your training, and let your love for the game show. Baseball is more than just a game; it's a community, a test of character, and a place to make experiences that will last a lifetime. Now is your chance to write your part of the incredible story of baseball. Grab your glove and go to bat. You're ready for the game that's coming up. Remember that the trip never ends; if you keep working hard and loving what you do, you'll be swinging for the fences for a long time.

www.ingramcontent.com/pod-product-compliance
Lightning Source LLC
Chambersburg PA
CBHW020257180726
47994CB00027B/1346